I Love Money,
But Does Money Love Me?

I Love Money,
But Does Money Love Me?

A radical change in one's attitude and relationship
in making progress towards financial freedom

Charles Phillips

To order additional copies of this book, contact:
Xlibris Corporation
1-888-795-4274
www.Xlibris.com
Orders@Xlibris.com
61565

Contents

PREFACE

MANY AFRICAN-AMERI-CANS, along with other ethic groups, are drawn to the Atlanta area, the "big apple city of the south" because of its Mecca image. You have an onslaught of young African-Americans and others settling in the area due to "prestigious" housings, employment, and the various lifestyles that allow the freedom to consume huge quantities of material things to impress others and to bring short term satisfactions. In reality, 2/3 of our country's economy is built on consumption and although we may not realize it, in the long haul, these "things" only diminish and depreciate. While Atlanta has its good points, it is also a very superficial city–for most, the real opportunities for true success are just not there and so, many are left with being concerned only with their outward appearances; such as their fashionable dress, the condition of their hair style, their cosmetic nails and facial makeup, their vacations, their perceived status, and the maintaining their cars and homes.

Although I can't say this about everybody, there are a lot of people, especially African-Americans, who have the mentality of wanting to have the nicest things that they can afford or not afford for that matter without any regards to the consequences of their actions. If we cannot change our attitude and relationship towards money and continue down the path of consumption, we will never be able to navigate through our economic system breakdown and will eventually be led into financial bondage.

> *Don't wear yourself out trying to get rich.*
> *Be wise enough to control yourself.*
> Proverbs 23:4

There's a story that goes like this, "A young man decided to take his wife and boisterous mother-in-law on a vacation to Israel. Unfortunately, while there, his mother-in-law passed away and so he was left with a decision to make. He could have her body shipped back home at a cost of $5,000 or he could have her buried in Jerusalem for $100. Well, he thought about it for a brief moment and decided to have her body shipped back home. You see, he had heard that some long time ago, a young man died and was buried in Jerusalem and after 3 days, rose from the dead. He felt that he just couldn't take the chance and have his mother-in-law do the same." Faulty information and personal feelings will many times determine our actions! I believe this often happens in the way we handle our finances.

In an illustrative and sometime humorous way, I hope to show the present state of this way of thinking that causes most, and especially, African-Americans and their households to get themselves into the trap of financial bondage. A question for you to ponder: "How are God's thoughts different from your thoughts on money?" Although this type of thinking behavior is not unique in the African-American community, I will focus here simply because of my experience and association with the community. However, I do want to say, financial bondage is not solely a curse among African-Americans, but a very real curse among all ethic groups.

Just to show how serious a problem we have, let me take a moment to tell quick story of a very good African-American friend, who recently wanted to borrow $60 dollars to pay his storage fees on the things he felt to be valuable and precious. You see he lived the good life, or so he thought, until he ran out of money to pay his enormous rent–he then had to move out and live in an extended stay motel. He had no savings, although he still drove an Escalade automobile. In trying to keep up the payments on his "things" he was always asking to borrow money–this time $60 dollars! Would you say he was somewhat concerned with maintaining his "things?" I would say yes!

Anyhow, back to my subject, by writing this book, I believe it will be an enlightenment to you through showing how with making radical changes in one's attitude and relationships towards the resources in their possession, and how by using the principles and biblical teachings of God, one can come out of financial bondage and live in a life of financial freedom with real assurances. You see, God is looking for people to help navigate through these economic times and He really want you to see the possibilities for making a difference, for contentment, and for freedom that you have never known before in living and handling your possessions. Paul in writing to Timothy told him to flee from the love of money and its harmful desires. We too, need to do the same thing.

ACKNOWLEDGMENTS

I WANT TO TAKE this time to thank the counselors and friends of the late Larry Burkett and Crown Ministries for patiently and persistently working with me to make the changes needed and giving me the track to run on to go from financial bondage to financial freedom. I also want to thank Dave Ramsey for his ministry in helping me to "be real" with the task. Many thanks to James and Sharon Vincent, along with Victory World Church, for giving me the opportunity to give back, in service, to others what God has instilled in me. A real shout out for my wife, Priscilla, who walked with me, even when at times it seemed as if I was going over the deep end. We experience some times of "intense fellowship" but in the end, we now agree it was well worth the trip. Most importantly, I thank God for His Word, His principles and methods, without which I would never have embarked on my journey to change.

Several of the quotations and notes used are from the word of God as presented by "The Everyday Bible-New Century Version"

For a selection of other financial Bible studies, contact Crown Financial Ministries at www.crown.org.

INTRODUCTION

WHILE GROWING UP I can not remember ever going without, but I do recall lights and phone being cut off, car being reposed, and bill collectors calling or dropping by. My father did what he had to do to keep us together and contented. He was good at it and my hero, but he did have a problem with handling his resources. As a result, I had no training or teaching on how to handle my finances properly, and so, lived a life of trying to keep up with "the Joneses"–I was very bad! At times I was dishonest, deceitful, and did not honor the Lord with the finances He had entrusted to me. All I did was seek the pleasures of this world–not so unlike countless other African-Americans. However, maybe not so much like all, but a large number of many, my way of living came to a crashing end when I lost everything. I lost my home, had my car repossessed, my salary garnished, liens put on my bank accounts, and credit ratings so low I couldn't even borrow a dime using a quarter as collateral. My bank accounts were always overdrawn, I had no savings, a negative net worth (not so bad since one-third of African-American households have no assets or a negative net worth), and several other negative situations due to poor handling of my finances. I owed more money than I could count to more people than I knew. More often than not,

I was flat broke and living from paycheck to paycheck! Enough was enough! When I was at rock bottom with no where to go nor no one to turn to, a good Christian friend approached me with an offer to get involved in presenting financial seminars to the various churches in his organization—The Christian and Missionary Churches. Even though my finances were a mess, I kept it a secret and still held some esteem within the church organization as being one of the very few African-American church treasurers. I decided to take him up on his offer, took training with "Larry Burkett Organization" and started giving financial seminars in Georgia and Florida. The more I did this, the more uneasy I felt about living a lie. I was telling others how to live right with their finances, yet I was living just the opposite. I had to make a change, not because I saw the light, but because I felt the heat! I tried the "get rich quick schemes", working two and three jobs, the lottery and other avenues, but none of them worked, I still was in bondage. Finally, I decided to confess to my Pastor and my Christian friend and to seek the Lord for help (this always seems to happen when you hit rock bottom). Being a member of a church and an active participant in the financial ministry, I did hear of the Lord's plan for success in handling your finances, so after a lot of prayer and a lot of meditating on His word, I came to realize that He did have a better plan for my life—one of peace, joy, and abundance. I made the decision to change my direction, changed my way of thinking, and started living a life according to the plan of God, free of dishonesty and deceit. My church, Pastor, and friend all worked closely with me. Now I'm not saying it was all that easy to change, I fell and stumbled many times but once I made up my mind to change and the change was made, I found it was much easier to live under God's economy rather than under the world's economy.

My journey is not so unlike others who made the change, but than maybe it is, you see, not only did I seek God's input, I also sought counsel with many Christian friends—those who had their act together. They were individuals, who handled their finances the way God told them to do so. They were solid and sincere in handling their finances in a Christian way by following the precepts of God. During one of my many counseling and budgeting sessions, I was introduced to and encouraged to take the Crown Biblical Financial Study Course and you know, I decided to take it. It was during this course, that I really began to make some serious changes in my way of thinking. I started living more and more according to God's economy. I saw myself, not as an owner, but as a steward of the resources God had for me. Living financially free, not in financial bondage was His system. It took some real determination, steady plodding on my part and a lot of encouragement to make the change, but with time, I changed and made some positive progress. I engage in less impulse buying, started giving, and began paying off my debts. Today my debts are all paid off (except my current home), and I have built a better than good savings account. But the most important thing to happen for me was that God began to prosper me not so that I would raise my standard of living, but so that I would raise my standard of giving.

> *You make a living by what you get–*
> *You make a life by what you give.*
> *Winston Churchill*

You see, God took a mess of a person like me and made into a productive one, so that today, He's able to use me as a Christian Budget Coach and a Crown Class Facilitator at my place of worship. With my new attitude and way of thinking on handling money, I'm now living a life of peace and contentment. I've also become a generous giver as God would want us all to be. Guess what? Along the way, I found out that "the Joneses" were just as broke as I was. It took a good portion of my adult life to get into this bondage, but as a word of encouragement, I want you to know that it did not take long to get into financial freedom. I just stop speaking, acting, and doing negative things. I started seeing those things that were not as if they were and doing the positive things of God. If He did it for me and countless others, I know He will do it for you!

All the people who don't know God keep trying to get these things.
And your Father in heaven knows that you need them.
The thing you should want most is God's kingdom and doing what God wants.
Then all these other things you need will be given to you.
Matthew 6:31-32

Your heart will be where your treasure is.
Matthew 6:21

MY MONEY . . . HUH?

I OWE, I OWE, and off to work I go! This is a very familiar quote of many. Others may say–it's a job that puts food on the table and pays my bills. Too many times, I've heard people say, "I got kids at home and a wife or husband to keep off my back". Either way you look at it, both are really dumb reasons for going to work and getting into and staying in debt! To do this for 30 or 40 years is just plain stupid! Yet, as African-Americans, we have brought into the lie of living in debt. Think about it, we are taught to focus on income accumulation to obtain things. It is our most single-minded challenge! We earn money day after day, month after month, year after year with no real plans on how to manage it. We have no plans on how to spend it, how to save it, or how to invest it! Yes we may think of our children's college education–just so that they can get a good job to buy things! But for most African-Americans this is only a dream with no feet to it. It's a game we play and is so easy to join in. There are several names for this game, but they all lead to the same result–a huge funnel emptying us into a life of debt! You may love money, but does money really love you? I'll give an example of one of the games we love to play. I'll call it the "Credit Card Challenge."

My Credit Card Game:

Early on in my adult life, I will never forget the day I went to the mailbox and found a new credit card in it. It was a new store card sent to me simply because they thought I was credit worthy. Of course, I wasn't sure if it was "real", but thought I would try it out anyhow, so I went to the store with, as *Lee Jenkins* says, my new "Massa's" card and $5.00 dollars in my pocket to purchase a hat for $3.95 ($5.00 was back up just in case the credit card was a fake). Well, the card was not a fake, I was able to use the card to charge the hat and I was on my way into a life of debt–"the good life!" I could now "own" things without having to pay for them up front. I guess you might say this was the beginning of a long and slow slide downward into my bondage of debt. Life seemed to be just too good for me. Other credit cards began to show up merely by asking. Material things began to appear in my possession merely by signing a slip of paper and I only had to use a small potion of my paycheck to pay for it. This is probably the primary way we find ourselves getting into debt bondage and not even realizing what we are doing to ourselves.

It is so easy to become a card-carrying member of the typical African-American household of very low net wealth, which incidentally for the average African-American household fell 32% in 2003 to $5788. Even worse, 29.4% of African-American households in 2004 had zero or negative net worth. But than "what is net worth?" In 2005, 48.2% of African-Americans owned homes slipping behind Hispanics who had a home ownership of 49.5%. Not only did I have very low net wealth, but I also had no reason to save (so I thought). Yes, I was part of the 45% of African-American households to be "wealthy poor", holding less than $10,000 in net wealth. I was also part of the 48% of African-Americans spending more than their income, and part of the 59% of African-Americans not saving on any regular basis at all. More frightening, I was part of the 70% of African-American households who lived from paycheck to paycheck and one of the 81% of African-American households that did not have a planning horizon of at least five years, neither short term or long term plans.[1]

With so much talent, gifts, knowledge, and wisdom in the African-American community, why do we, as a group, rank lowest in financial freedom and highest in financial bondage? When you look at the statistics, one can not help but to wonder just how as African-Americans we have such a mindset when it comes to handling our finances. Just what are the statistics telling us? Well, first as a group, we are shown to control a very sizable percentage of the country's wealth and have over 892 Billion dollars of buying power which is forecast to over 1.1 Trillion by 2012! Out of this wealth, we gave 9.2 Billion to charities and spent in telephone services alone 12.3 Billion. So, it's not that we do not have wealth to control, but rather how we manage it. Here in lies one of the problems–how we manage our wealth! Take a typical African-American household, they will earn approximately $39,200 per year (the lowest among all racial groups) and will not have a written spending plan (I like this over saying a budget) to live by and therefore will spend 78% of this income for housing and transportation (which is too much) leaving very little or no income to do any thing else without the use of credit. 42% of us will not have any savings, and 47% of us will be unwilling to take financial risks by investing. What is so shocking, our median net worth is less than $6,000 as compared to over $112,000 for White America. Of course a lot of this behavior has to do with the financial education African-Americans receive and this is another problem we have. Although many of us go to college and study hard, we mainly focus on the end results and not the journey. Although most of our career climb is long and slow, we keep working at it with the hope that one day we will look up and see that things have changed for the better–*the end result*. We will no longer drive a car that sprays gray smoke, we will go out to dinner a few times per year and maybe take vacations–we would have, as some may say, "Come a long ways baby!" Yet, we will still be in debt!–*The journey*. You may ask, "What's so bad about debt?" Isn't everybody in debt? Aren't companies, city and state governments in debt? Our own federal government owes over 15 Trillion dollars in debt or put another way, about $134,000 per each man, woman, and child in this United States. Even churches are in debt, and so, what's the big issue????? The issue is that debt is a cruel and vice gripping trap!

When you look at all the adjectives used for debt you see words like: *liable, owing, due, in the red, in arrears, in hock, minus, outstanding, broke.* When you look at this list, you see nothing positive, all negative, so, asked another way, what's good about debt?

It is not always a lack of money that creates financial pressure. Many times it is simply a matter of attitude. There is a right attitude towards money (Gods way) and a wrong attitude (mans way). You see, money and material things is not the problem, it is the use of money and the attitude towards it that is the problem. Freedom from debt can be accomplished with a changed attitude. Ask yourself this question: "What is the hardest area of your thinking/life you content with and really feel need changing?"

> *The love of money causes all kinds of evil. Some people have left*
> *the true faith because they want to get more and more money,*
> *but they have caused themselves much sorrow.*
> 1Timothy6:10

God warns us to guard our hearts against greed, ego, and pride, because these are emotional tools and behaviors that control us. He also want us to see that believing all the money that I have as being *mine*, puts me under the control of money, rather than the other way around. If it's *mine*, than it exist to serve me and for a Christian, that is a path towards sin and selfishness. In the area of finances, African-Americans are extremely vulnerable to these emotional tools. These tools appear to explain the differences between African American household wealth and White American wealth. They, more than most other ethnic groups, need constant encouragement to follow the steps that will ensure money management according to God's plan in order to assure financial freedom in their lives. Now, I know receiving this encouragement from others, especially African-Americans may be rare for several reasons. First most of our African-American families do not leave an inheritance, just don't have any, so as a result, we get no encouragement to protect the family wealth. Second, many African-Americans come from impoverished families that had very little income to handle–thus managing was only to the extent of paying for the bare necessities, again, really no reason for encouragement. There are other reasons and I'm sure you can think of some, but in short, we need to get through all of them if we indeed are to help each other onto the road of financial freedom.

The person who loves money will never have all the money he wants,
The person who loves wealth will not be satisfied when he gets it.
This is also useless.
Ecclesiastes 5:10

COUNTING THE COST/ GOOD JUDGEMENT

WOULD YOU BUY a house if you were allowed to see only one of its rooms? Would you purchase a car if you were permitted to see only its tires? Would you past judgment on a book after reading only one paragraph? Chances are you would say no. Yet the opposite is true for the vast majority of African-Americans when it comes to handling their finances.

Good judgment or counting the cost requires a broader picture. Not only is it true in purchasing houses, cars, and books, it's also true in handling your finances. Let's look at some areas we have problems with and I will start with a story of my nephew Kenny:

Kenny's Story:

Kenny went and purchased a newer used car. He came to me with what he thought was "a good deal". He brought a new used car! Here's how he explained it to me, he was able to trade in his 2000 Economy Car for a 2001 Luxury Car, the dealer rolled over the remaining balance on his older car into the new loan. He was able to get the loan for a five year period with monthly payments of only $401, saving himself $134 per month. He owed $3400 on the older car and at just over $500 per month, had about eight more payments to make. He now has sixty $400 payments totaling $24000. Why did he think this was such a good deal for him? Well, he did cut his monthly payments from just over $500 to $400, a savings of $100 per month. Did the total cost of this transaction play any role in his decision? Did the thought of paying $24000 for a car worth no more than $4400 ever cross his mind? It never did! This type of behavior amplifies the financial ignorance of many African-Americans. Why do you think so many auto dealers advertise car sales and loans showing boldly monthly payments only, almost never will you see advertisements showing interest rates of 21%–28%, or that one could pay more in interest than the cost of the car? He did not understand the fine print or details and was hurt when I said it was a "baaaad" deal and disagreed with him.

The average car retains only about 35 percent of its original value after a five-year ownership period. Why is this so important to know? Most African-Americans are upside on their car loans, meaning they owe more than the car is worth. What is so troubling is that when they trade in the car, they still owe on average more than $3,600. What happens to this balance? Well it is rolled over into another often much higher loan. [2]

If you want to build a tower,
you first sit down and decide how much it cost.
Luke 14:28

Another area we are trapped in using poor judgment is the trap of–**Materialism.**

The majority of African-Americans are really locked in the bondage of materialism, a really bad habit! Let me tell you how this habit really affects us.

Our Story:

My wife and I took a cruise to the Mexican Rivera and upon our return at disembarkation, my suitcase was missed placed. We spent a short time looking for it, since we had to catch a flight home; all we could do was to fill out a lost baggage form. Needless to say, I was somewhat upset; all I could think of was my new leather cap and two new souvenir tee shirts I had just bought and never worn. However, I quickly got over the loss and started counting the days until I would receive a $1000 check in the mail. Figured I could replace my loss with brand new clothing. Since I had not brought any new clothing in over three years, I had no Idea that $1000 would not replace all of my losses. I had no insurance coverage (you know a waste of money). Anyhow, I had to wait ten days for settlement, and would you believe it, my suitcase arrived at my home on the eight day! Again, I am very upset, no new clothes! Now my thought process goes like this, these clothes were over three years old, they were out dated and suddenly I had no more use for them, I needed new and in style clothes! It took awhile for me to calm down and begin thinking rational again. Was the new hat so valued and important to upset me so, were my clothes really so out dated, or was that material habit trying to raise it ugly head again? Yes, I went through eight days of "highs and lows" being driven by the demonic material habit, oh yes, it is a demon! Am I the only one being driven? I don't think so, it affects African-Americans so much so, and that we tolerate and justify our living in excessive debt by not counting the cost or using good judgment when making decisions to spend. Put another way, by not using good judgment, African-Americans, too often, spend money in seeking wealth for enjoyment and pleasure. Since this is often short lived, they have very little to show to justify their spending.

As Dr William Darity, professor of African American studies at Duke University says; "If African Americans would engage in less impulse buying and save more, wealth disparities could be eliminated."

I have learned to be satisfied with the things
I have and with everything that happens.
Philippians 4:11b

Let's look at another area of poor judgment that traps us–**Planning and Setting Goals.** First, my question to you is this: How are you with managing time or with planning and setting goals? If you are like most African-Americans, you probably don't have any written plans or goals and to take the time to pause for a moment and put a name to every dollar you bring in is just too troublesome. Our lack in this area is another bad situation we find ourselves in. I know, you are saying you don't need to, you already know where the dollars are going–to pay bills! It's sad, but most African-Americans operate in this mode of thinking–70% of African-Americans live paycheck to paycheck just paying bills. Our habits are well established and if you are like most, you find it difficult, if not impossible to change your ways–especially in handling "your money".

As I looked back over my own personal experiences, I realized that I didn't make changes until the "pain of remaining the same" became greater than the "pain of change". You see, I was like so many others, I just could not see any benefits in planning, especially when my money was funny (got that from *Lee Jenkins*) or the bills had piled high. If things came up, I handle them as I could, I begged, borrowed, or stole from "Peter to pay Paul!" I think of the first vacation I ever took, I went to The Bahamas and had a great time. I spent up all my money and hated to leave. The problem with this vacation was that I came back and was not able to pay my rent. The thought never crossed my mind to plan on setting aside some money to pay for a place to live. You see my next one or two paychecks would take care of that, at the time my only plan. Now I know many of you may not carry your lack of planning this far, but lack of planning to any extent can be very harmful. What if I didn't get those paychecks? What about those other expenses, oh they just go un-paid for a while. Because I didn't plan, I was always falling behind and playing catch up. I lived this way for years and finally had to ask myself the question, "Why am I living this kind of lifestyle and why won't I change it?" Maybe I just don't know any different, maybe my attitude and relationship is just all off centered. It's really amazing just how we can make excuses for or justify our behavior. Really though, the answer was always there for me. I as with so many others was just disobedient towards the teachings of God and deeply entrenched in the worlds system of handling resources.

Those who plan and work hard earn a profit.
But those who act too quickly become poor.
Proverbs 21:5

SOUNDS FAMILIAR?

L ET'S LOOK AT some other crazy things we do to get ourselves into bondage. Now you need money to pay those other bills–so, where do you get it? How about Payday Loans, Oh yes! You can pay it back next payday. All you need is a checking account and a job. Done deal! One small problem, you have other bills to pay, so when payday comes around, you can't pay the loan! So you pay the interest, 100–200% or some astronomical figure you are really clueless about. This can go on for months and by the time they are finished with you, say you borrowed $100 you probably will have paid them back $600. SOUNDS FAMILIAR?

How about those student loans? Did you know you could use them to live off while in school? After all, we are really too lazy to search for grants or to keep our grades up to be able to qualify for scholarships so we just take loans and when we graduate and get a good job, then we'll pay the loans back. Oh no, you are part of the 46% of students who don't complete their schooling. Now you got to pay those loans and guess what, you really don't have such a great job to do so! But so you do graduate, is the job you do get really that great–I mean to pay off those loans and spend and live the way you really want to? SOUNDS FAMILIAR?

What about car loans? This is really sad what we do. Buy here, pay here, you know your credit is shot and although you paid for the car when you drove it off the lot, you still got to make weekly payments—forever! SOUNDS FAMILIAR?

But then maybe your credit is not in the toilet, but it's not that great either, don't feel bad, you are not alone, a very large number of people have bad credit. Anyhow, you go to a car dealership and get this great deal, you pay a $513 monthly car note on a car valued at around $25,000. Let's say your rate of interest is 8.5%, you will make this monthly payment for five years and end up with a car valued at just under $6,000. Understand this note does not include insurance, maintenance, or gasoline payments. These payments can easily double your monthly note. But then, as so many don't, you really didn't plan on this extra expense! SOUNDS FAMILIAR?

Want to talk about home loans? The county I live in is now 95% African-American (it was 50-50 when I first moved into the county) the foreclosure rate is the 197th highest in the country. Many used ARMs and "interest-only" loans to buy homes priced way over their heads. Then the rates changed! Unemployment rose and now most of the current homeowners are in homes that have decreased in value by 18.5% from 2007 to 2008 leaving many financially strapped and unable to afford their mortgages on homes that are owed more than what they are worth. African-Americans are hit the hardest. They are three times more likely to have sub prime loans, which account for 55% of all the loans to them. They account for 80% of the foreclosures in the county. Do you think, just maybe, this foreclosure freefall of many African-Americans has something to do with all of these creative loans, rate changes, and unemployment? SOUNDS FAMILIAR?

Then there are the credit cards for those of us who can get them. This country has a method in place to keep you in debt; it's called "plan obsolescent and technological advancement". African-Americans really buy into it. We need the latest, newest, biggest, and best of everything. We put it on the credit card and then make the minimum payments. A little known fact most of us don't think about is this, With an average family credit card balance of over $9,000 and with the minimum payment used by most, it will take an average of 23 years to pay off and cost over $6,600 in interest charges, but then—so what if it takes a life time to pay it off. A survey was taken and found that 92% of the respondents said credit cards are a necessity and 35% of them held 5 or more credit cards. Their average credit card debt amounted to 8.5% of income. Again, I ask, why do we need to carry so many credit cards and such a high debt load? SOUNDS FAMILIAR?

These are just a few of the crazy things we do to keep ourselves in financial bondage. I could go on with some others, but I think you have a feel of where I'm going with this. Can we honestly say we enjoy this, that we are happy, and that this is the only way to live?

Please help me find something good about debt. Personally I can not see anything good about destroying lives, families, and whole communities. We do a lot to impress others, but I really believe our way of impressing others is all wrong! We are the greatest debtor nation in world history—The United States. As African Americans we contribute greatly to this trend. We say we are Americans and believe we can/will solve our economic money problems, however, the reality is 2/3 of our country's economy is built on consumption and we don't realize we are moving into a moral and social breakdown. It's been said, that there are two ways to conquer and enslave a people: One is by the sword, the other is by debt. If we are to avoid this, we need to turn from our ways and allow God to navigate us through our economic chaos.

When a person sees danger ahead, he avoids it.
But a foolish person keeps going and gets into trouble.
Proverb 22:3

CHANGE IS IN ORDER

WITH AN AVERAGE earning of $25,000, one will earn over $1,000,000 in a lifetime, however, that same person will have spent most or all of it and retire with next to nothing. Why is this end the result of so many? I believe it is due to poor judgment, bad decisions, and entrenchment in this world's economy. Again, I want to say that this problem of financial miss-management and being in debt is not just limited to the African-American, but to all racial groups, however, to know that 70% of African-Americans live paycheck to paycheck and 48% of them are in debt, as an African-American I feel an urgency and obligation to address the African-American community. If you are not an African-American, please don't close the book and walk away, the solutions I will set forth, can be applied by you too. You too can become financially free. *3*

A foolish person thinks he is doing right,
But a wise person listens to advice.
Proverbs 12:15

As I mentioned in my introduction, I mishandled the resources of God badly, I hit rock bottom and I guess you can say was forced to change my ways; form new attitudes, new dreams, and new directions. You may not hit rock bottom as I did, but you may look in a mirror and not be impressed with what you see or you may hear a small voice that is not impressed with you. You just might be reminded that none of what you accumulate in life matters if it accrues only to benefit you and yours at the cost of being in debt! These uneasy feelings may, just maybe, cause you as with me to begin to see doing things in a different way. Now I know, you may ponder these feelings for months without answers and/or with out making a move to change, but then, there's always that feeling of not being all or doing all one is capable of being or doing. There just seems to always be something missing in life. I believe that something is one not being in the will of God when it comes to His resources. However, if a person has the desire to live the life God has for them and move with confidence in the direction of that desire, knowing that God is on their side, they will progress and meet with great success. However, most of us fail to move on our desires because we are out of God's will and in the bondage of debt. Most African-Americans do not have clearly in their minds what they want, what they are to do, what they are to know, or what their purpose is in God's plan for their lives. Because of this lack of knowledge, we mostly strike out on our own following those shadow goals set by others or society. This happens so many times with so many people, even in my own life. I'll give you another personal example;

My Story:

I went to college to become a Psychologist. After several stops and starts I ended up coming out of school with a major in Sociology. I could not deal with some of the courses I needed to be a Psychologist and settled for Sociology simply because I had a family to support. I had no real concrete goals, except for the ones set for me by society which were to get a college education so that I could get a high paying job. Well, I didn't get that great paying job and because I had no idea what God's plan was for me, I quickly drifted into a life of buying things I didn't need, with money I didn't have, to impress people I really didn't like. I was in the vicious cycle of working, wanting, and buying stuff. Unknowingly I was keeping up with "the Joneses", not realizing they were just as broke as I was! What was so sad about all of this, I did it for a number of years! Oh yes, I moved up from driving a car that laid down a smoke screen to a brand new car with air condition and a tape deck. I went from an apartment to a house with a basement, took vacations, brought my kids just about all the "things" they wanted or what I thought they needed. However, I gave no money to anyone, owed a considerable amount of money and had less than $200 dollars in savings. I was living in a state of discontentment from paycheck to paycheck thinking I was doing OK. When, really, I was quite unhappy!

Webster's New Collegiate Dictionary defines **discontentment** as:
A restless aspiration for improvement–disillusionment–frustration–uneasiness–aimlessness

Many people live a life of discontentment, take billionaire *Howard Hughes*, when he died, naked and terrified of flies; someone asked "how much did he leave?" The answer was, "all of it!" You see, he ended his life in a state of disillusion, afraid to venture out into public, although he had billions of dollars. Many of us end our lives in a state of disillusion and broke! I'm not saying everyone end up this way, but there are so many that do.

Let's take a moment and pause in thoughts. We all would like to have millions of dollars, but we don't. God would not give it to most of us because we would not know how to handle it and besides, for most, He could not trust us with it anyhow! You may find it difficult to accept, but if you are really honest with yourself, there are areas in your life that do need to be changed in order for you to get a small raise, much less a million dollars. I know I had several changes to make. I did not like the road I was taking and I'm so thankful that I made the changes.

Ask yourself this question: "How do I see myself handling and spending the money God gives to me?" If your answer is that you are not doing it His way, then you have a real problem. Your first step should be to change your attitude and relationship with His money and how you handle it. Second, you must really know and believe that there is nothing, absolutely nothing good about debt and at all cost should be avoided! You got to see it as a cruel and unmerciful enemy that need to be destroyed. You really do need to understand and know just how controlling and bad debt really is. Look at it this way, it forces us into slavery (every dollar we earn we owe four), it destroys family values (we are always arguing, working and sliding away from God); it hinders the gospel (I can't tithe or give and pay my debts).

Should you change your thinking, change your base? Put another way, should you stop using the world's way of thinking as your base and start using God's way as your base. If you think on this, you will come to realize the right answer is **yes!** This step is probably the most difficult one for you to make, but it is vital that you do so! You must change your thinking in order for you to prosper and have good success. God cannot trust you with finances if you are always in debt! How we handle His resources tells who we worship.

You know, God knew before hand that the area of finances would be the area of great problems in our lives. Many Christians are surprised to learn that approximately two-thirds of the parables that Christ used in teaching deal specifically with money. There are over 2350 bible verses dealing with handling money, so you see God, our creator, the author of all things really knows how we should handle the money He entrusts to each one of us. On the other hand, Satan is an expert on taking our greed, ego, and pride, and using them as tools to control and manipulate us in this world. Because of this, debt is alive and well in our world and we are beaten down most of the time with it. But what is really needed is to beat Satan down, and to do so, we need to be taught God's word on finances clearly and undiluted. Then we need to take the next step and go out and demonstrate that Satan can not continue to manipulate us–That God's ways really do work.

Lord you are great and powerful. You have glory,
victory and honor. Everything in heaven and on earth belongs to you.
The kingdom belongs to you, Lord. You are the ruler over everything.
1 Chronicles 29:11

What kind of control does the world's economy have on us? Well let's take a look at Jimmy as an example:

Jimmy O's Story:

> Jimmy could not wait to graduate from high school and get a job. Well he did graduate and got his job. His first action after receiving his first paycheck was to spend it in getting his first car. His next 100 or so paychecks were used in part to pay for the car. Along the way he brought other things, clothing, jewelry, electronics, etc . . . He really felt as if he was living the life, especially after seeing how credit could acquire him the things he wanted without having the money on hand.–Like a frog in a pot of water, by turn the heat up slowly and he never realized he was slowly being cooked to death.

Likewise, our world has shaped our way of thinking so much so that most of us really believe it is the only way to live. We don't realize, or for some believe, that there is another way–God's way. We say and believe that being in debt, spending, no saving, and not giving to others is the way of life in this world and to do otherwise is just not American. We have forgotten the mantra; "Use it up, wear it out, make it do, or do without!"

During the great depression of 1930, people saved butter wrappers to grease pans, filled drawers with empty bread bags, washed foil paper to use again. For most of us today, such thriftiness would be amusing. Today, we throw away nearly everything in sight. We are living in a throw away society–to be thrifty is just not "cool." We are just too manipulated to think any other way. Jimmy is like countless numbers of African-Americans who have been taught that happiness comes only from earning and spending money to get the "things" of this world.

Well, it was hard, but in my case, I decided to stopped being manipulated and started demonstrating. How did I do it? First, I had to admit it's hard to break old habits and to change ones way of thinking, but it is not impossible! Second, I had to take time in solitude to take stock and get real with my situation. I had to ask some hard questions of myself, such as:

- How do I want to be remembered?
- How much money is enough?
- What do I want for my family?
- Do I really like being in debt?
- Am I living a balanced life?

Finally, before I could tackle specific financial strategies and goals, I had to seek some spiritual counseling to get some sound answers.

Lord, examine me and know my heart; Test me and know my thoughts.
See if there is any bad thing in me. Lead me in the way you set long ago.
Psalm 139:23-24

What I'm about to say is not all that new—probably have been said before, but I and so many others have eternalized these following steps and as a result, now experience financial freedom. You will never know that the life you are now living can be different, that your belief in this world system can be changed, without first taking these steps. Doing so will put you on the road to making some real changes in your life for the better. I can only ask that you too will consider taking these steps towards financial freedom. Really, change your thought patterns and really consider the steps I'm putting forth to you!

A foolish person thinks he is doing right,
but a wise person listens to advice.
Proverbs 12:15

THE STEPS

THESE ARE THE steps, and to make it clearer, I will outline them in the order to be taken:

First . . .

- <u>You must get God involved.</u>

You need to get God involved in the problem. After all, all the money is His anyway. The earth and everything in it, the world and all who live in it is His. God wants to help us get rid of the word *mine* when it comes to money. We need to think of our money not as ours, but rather as what it truly is—HIS! You see, the word *mine* is so deeply embedded in us that it takes a significant act of God to get it out of us. God want to free us from money's bondage and help us put it in its proper place by considering it His rather than ours. He wants this to happen in our hearts, not as some kind of rule or regulation. He wants us to be so grateful for what he has done for us in Jesus that we understand the freedom of allowing all our possessions to be His.

The earth and everything in it belong to the Lord
Psalm 24:1

Second . . .

- You must get wisdom.

You really need wisdom before you need money, for without it you will not know how to properly manage money. Think for a moment; do you have a "coach", "confident", "comrade", "confronter"? This could be one or more persons to speak into your life? If not, why not?

It is better to get wisdom than gold.
It is better to choose understanding than silver.
Proverbs 16:16

Third . . .

- You must get real.

The concept of *mine* comes naturally. According to early childhood professionals, the words *my* and *mine* begin to emerge by 18 months of age. We take credit for a lot instead of giving God the credit. Think of your material possessions or accomplishments, how many of them have you taken credit for, rather than thanking God for? You got to acknowledge your way of thinking about possessions and debt and recognize that poor control of your finances put you into the debt trap.

Pay attention and listen to what wise people say.
Remember what I am teaching you.
Proverbs 22:17

As I mentioned, your first step is to take refuge in God and make the decision to start now to move and get out of debt. By doing so, you will start demonstrating and stop being manipulated.

When we read the calling of the boy Samuel we see that Samuel did not yet know the Lord so when the Lord called, he at first thought it was his mentor Eli. This is how the story goes: "In the days of Samuel, God did not speak directly to people very often. There were very few visions, but one night while Samuel was laying in bed, God called him. He answered, "I am here" and ran to Eli, his mentor. But Eli said, "I didn't call you, go back to bed." God called again, and again Samuel ran to Eli. Again Eli said, "I didn't call you, go back to bed. Now God called Samuel a third time, and again Samuel went to Eli and said, "I am here, you called me." Then Eli realized it was God calling Samuel. So he told Samuel to go to bed and said to him: "if God calls you again, say, speak Lord. I am your servant and I am listening. Then Eli said, "He is the Lord. Let him do what he thinks is best." Then the Lord came and stood there. He called as he had before. He said, "Samuel, Samuel!" Samuel said, "Speak, Lord. I am your servant, and I am listening." Samuel listened to the Lord and did all He said. Then the Lord was with Samuel as he grew up. He did not let any of Samuel's messages fail to come true and all of Israel knew Samuel was a prophet of the Lord."[4]

For many of us, as Samuel did, we need to make the decision to listen and do what the Lord says—change our attitude and relationship with "our money" and start seeing it as God's money. No longer are you the owner and controller, but now you must become a manager or steward over your finances—you don't own anything! Here is where I probably lose a lot of you, where many of you walk away—just can not think of giving up control or settling on God's money, not "my money." However, if you really want to change, you must make this first step, no matter how hard it may be. You must get God involved! You got to do some things you may have rarely done before, like praying. Understand, God will play a major role in helping you, but He got to become your closes partner. In going to Him, you are now asking for His advice and telling Him your problems. You also need to start listening to Him by reading His word, the Bible, to hear what He has to say. I know, for those of you who seldom or rarely read your Bible, this may be stretching it a bit, but Just do it! What He has to say will inspire you and change your life. I know this to be a fact, because He did it for me. So start reading, start praying and allow God to move in your life to make those changes needed. A note of caution, it may not seem as if anything is happening at first, but God is working and making the changes. For some of us, making the change is a little more difficult, but here are some hints to make this change a little easier. First, when it comes to praying, you can do that just about anytime. Keep it short and do so frequently through out the day. Second, when it comes to reading the Bible, you may not want to do so at bed time; it just might be the quickest way to put you to sleep. I found out the hard way, tried reading before I went to sleep and quickly discovered it was a sleeping pill, so I changed and set some time for reading during the day. What I'm saying to you is to make some immediate changes, however, as *Dave Ramsey* says, "stupid is not illegal" and you can continue your stupid ways of handling your resources.

Those individuals and families who submerged themselves in the Bible to see what God had to say, who after all created and put in place all of mankind and its systems and is the owner of everything, found themselves living the life of contentment we all seek. Although stupid is not illegal, it is definitely not life fulfilling. Following are just a couple of things the Lord has to say about all of this.

The silver is mine, and the gold is mine," says the Lord of Hosts.
Haggai 2:8

The land belongs to me.
You are only foreigners and travelers living for a time on my land.
Leviticus 25:23

Once I got started, I found it not very difficult to follow many of the teachings I found in the Bible and what I got out of reading other books. However, prior to that and not being a reader, and then having to read books on handling money, living out of debt, and accumulating wealth seemed to me as for other African-Americans a burdensome way to go, why not just play the lottery. All I had to do was hit the lottery and all my problems would be solved. The problem was I never hit the lottery! But you know, I just made up my mine to start reading, talking, and seeking the wisdom of others. Maybe it was hitting rock bottom and really not having any other way to go, but the more wisdom I received the more I realized that there was another and better way to live.

People handle money one of three ways: they spend less than they make and save money, or they break even, or they spend more than they make and go into debt. Sad to say, but 48% of African–Americans chose the latter way. This is something to think about! African-Americans will earn and control over 800 Billion dollars this year, and will spend 41% of that buying "things." Things that will depreciate in value over a period of time! Yet we insist on living this way and if we take away our houses, we have little or no accumulation of wealth. [5]

> *I have often said that the sole cause of man's unhappiness is that he does not know how to stay quietly in his room . . . . What people want is not the easy peaceful life that allows us to think of our unhappy condition, nor the dangers of war, nor the burdens of office, but the agitation that takes our mind off it and diverts us. That is why men are so fond of hustle and bustle; that is why the pleasures of solitude are so incomprehensible.*
>
> *Pascal*

We are really too busy, and as Pascal said, I just wonder what would really happen if we did take the time to sit still and ponder our situation? Would you come to grips with the mess you have made of yourselves? Well, for most of us, we do need to do so; we really need to come to grips with the mess we have made of ourselves. We really need to assess our lifestyles and come to realize it is NOT the way God intended for it to be. Perhaps if I told you a few stories of people just like you and how they took time to ponder and the affects on their lives by changing, you just might get a better understanding of what I'm saying.

Greg and Ellen's story:

Greg is a Salesman and Ellen is a Medical worker, they earn a very good salary together, more than $125,000, they have two car payments of more than $1500 per month, home mortgage of $1200 per month, over $21,000 in credit card debts, children in after school activities, 401K's, but no emergency fund and no savings. Each month, money came in and money went out. When there was a shortage, the credit cards were used. For 11 years they lived this way paying out all of their monies each month for "things" and never considering living out of debt. You see the world's way says it is OK to live in debt from paycheck to paycheck and to do so for 30–40 years!! However, Greg and Ellen said "NO", I got that from the movie "Planet of the Apes" when Cecil said "NO". They took a class on "handling money God's way"–it changed their whole way of thinking. They decided to do it God's way, to do what was taught to them. They were determined to try and handle their monies differently. As Greg will tell you, it wasn't easy, but the small victories kept them focused and on the right track. It took some time, but today they have no credit card debt, no car payments, an emergency fund set in place, and money saved in the bank–all because they changed their attitude and relationship to handling money.

Cathy W's story:

Cathy felt really guilty about not giving more to her church and to helping others. Her solution was a little easier, after some deep mediation on one of her pastor's sermons, she decided on obedience to God and started giving more and spending less. You know, it just happens that the more you give, the less you spend. If we left the story here, some of you would probably say "good for her" but her real reward from being obedient to God was that as time went by, God gave her more and more to give and still took care of all her needs. God blessed her for being obedient.

In my reading of God's Word, He clearly spoke in a way that settled the issue for me. You see, you just can't serve two masters at the same time; you will either love one or hate the other. I've come to believe that it is impossible to operate in both economies at the same time. You cannot serve God and money at the same time. It's like light and darkness cannot be in the same room at the same time. The world's economy and Gods economy are complete opposites of each other. The world's economy says it is OK to have debt–it encourages it! God's economy says *"do not owe people anything. But you will always owe love to each other."* Romans 13:8. The people who don't know God keep trying to get "things", but rather than wanting more "things", the thing you should want most is God's kingdom and doing what God wants. When we fail to do this, we bring on discontentment, anxiety, physical aliments, and a host of other unpleasant things. But by doing what God wants, He will give you all the things you need and also give you peace, joy, and contentment.

> *Do not store treasures for yourselves here on earth. Moths and rust will destroy treasures here on earth. And thieves can break into your house and steal the things you have. So store your treasure in heaven. The treasures in heaven cannot be destroyed by moths or rust. And thieves cannot break in and steal that treasure. Your heart will be where your treasure is.*
> Mathew 6:19-21

> *Then Jesus said to them, "Be careful and guard against all kinds of greed. A man's life is not measured by the many things he owns."*
> Luke 12:15

No servant can serve two masters.
He will hate one master and love the other.
Or he will follow one master and refuse to follow the other.
You cannot serve both God and money.
Luke 16:13

DECISIONS, DECISIONS

FOR MOST OF us, change only occur when; "the pain of remaining the same becomes greater than the pain of change." However, there is another way to help you consider making the change—the benefits!

At a very young age, Ezra diligently studied and learned to become a scholar. He won the respect of many, including the political leader of the land of his exile, King Artaxerxes. Ezra kept himself busy doing God's work while in exile. He established his connections and influence over time and as a result of many years of consistently doing the right thing, the king finally trusted Ezra with great power and resources. You see Ezra decided to do what was right in the Lord's eyesight and although he was in exile, he was greatly rewarded by the Lord.[6]

Let's take a look at a couple of stories of those receiving the benefits from making the change:

John B's story:

John B. gave small amounts to his church mission program. He wanted to give more, but because of his spending habits, never had extra money to give. He was living in the world's economy and only gave what he had left over. But then he was introduced to God's economy. He finally had a breakthrough. He wanted to know more of God's way and to live a life that was pleasing to Him. So with determination, he switched to God's economy and started to give out of his first fruits, changed his spending habits, and put the Lord first in his life. As in Cathy W. case, the Lord blessed him with an increase in his wealth so that he was able to give more and still take care of all his needs. God is true to His Word, He will change your situations for the better!

Marcus A's story:

Marcus A. was laid off from his job. During his time in searching for another job, he too had a change in his thinking and of his heart. I guess he felt the "heat"! He put the Lord first in his life and eventually found another job. This time he lived in God's economy. Three months after becoming debt free, he was again laid off, but this time, things were different, he did not have the stress and he was at peace, knowing that now he was a steward of God's resources and that God was in control. God quickly blessed him with another job at a higher income. But God is so good! He provided for Marcus' every need during the time he was unemployed.

*Whoever can be trusted with small things
can also be trusted with large things.*
Luke 16:10

I need to pause here for a moment. For many of you, your first step towards changing is to admit you don't have a personal relationship with God and that you want to make Jesus Christ your personal Lord and Savior. Many of you may say "I know God, or I believe in Jesus". You may even say you are a Christian, but you really cannot get God's involvement without first forming a personal relationship with His Son, Jesus Christ, making Him your personal Lord and Savior. I'm sure many of you know the difference between knowing someone and having a relationship with someone. For those of you needing this step, take this time to consider your relationship and those sins or sin you have and now want to confess to the Lord. If you really want to change and rebuild your life, then you need a clean heart and a real and true desire to form a spiritual and heartfelt relationship with God.

This is a short prayer you can say with real meaning from your heart:

> *Heavenly Father, in Jesus' name I repent of my sins and open my heart to let Jesus come inside of me. Jesus, you are my Lord and Savior. I believe you died for my sins and you were raised from the dead. Fill me with your Holy Spirit. Thank you, Father, for saving me in the name of Jesus. Amen.*

By saying the above prayer, you have committed your life to Christ and have formed a Christian relationship with God. Praise God! This is a short prayer of faith. You may doubt your belief in this truth because of the habitual direction of your life, but rests assure God is faithful and can be trusted fully to bless you. Areas of your life may and will give you trouble, however, you now need to trust God at all times and give your full attention to what He is doing right now in your life. Do not get upset about what happened or what may or may not happen tomorrow, God will help you to do what is right! God can and will help you to change–to become much more secured and stronger than you once were, so, just believe! The Apostle Paul wrote: "*Yes, I know that nothing good lives in me–I mean nothing good lives in the part of me that is earthly and sinful. I want to do the things that are good. But I do not do them.*" Romans 7:18. Remember, God will provide and protect you simply because He loves you and want to see you prosper and have good success. Take a look at this next story to see as an example, how God really do love you. This is CJ's story:

CJ's story:

CJ always played the Lottery–never won big but held great faith in knowing that one day he would hit it big. He never paid his bills on time, loved his beer and cigarettes. He never gave of "his money" to anyone. Somewhere during his journey, he had an encounter with the Lord and changed his life. He started to think differently–he now pays his bills on time and gives generously with the monies God provides to him. Occasionally he will still play the lottery and drink a beer or two, but he is growing in the ways of the Lord and living more and more in His economy. CJ realizes his resources and reputation belong to God and what he does with it will or will not glorify God.

We put too much faith in the "almighty dollar" and although God is patient with us, one just have to look at what's happening with today's economy and really believe that God is moving in a direction that will force those of us who have not decided to make a change, to indeed change our ways! Look at the current mortgage meltdown and credit crunch. Our greed and drive to keep up with the "Joneses", who's broke, has led us to a housing crisis unlike any we have seen. Home values are plummeting, foreclosures are now running 1 out of 10 homes and all due to the creative loan and mortgage practices that have suck in so many individuals, especially African-Americans, who simply could not afford and/or should not have been given the mortgages. The desire to have bigger and better "homes", and the easiness of "no doc" loans, most being deceitful by the lenders and flat out lies by the borrowers, have created such a mess in the housing market, that it will take years to correct. Next we have the use of credit cards and debit cards with their high interest rates and countless penalties that have entrapped thousands, again mostly African-Americans, to go deeper into debt. When we look at the federal government's debt of over 15 Trillion dollars, with the real possibility of adding another 2 Trillion dollars this year alone, it is easy to see how the general public falls right in step. It is really sad to see just how much control this world's economy has on us, so much so, that we as a current generation create debt with no intentions of repaying, rather leaving the repayment option to the future generations—our children and grandchildren. What's even more frightening, not only will they pay our debts, but also be burden with taking care of us in our "old" age simply because we cannot and will not save money due to our lifestyle of greed and debt. Just how fair is it to burden our children with our irresponsible behavior? How fair is it to teach our children the same habits and irresponsibility?

Train a child to live right. When he is old, he will still live that way.
Proverb 22:6

The treasures we seek after are not eternal. We stay in our homes 5–7 years (today's present circumstances may cause us to stay longer). Many drive the same car 3-5 years, then trade for a newer one. Things become obsolete, in some cases, within months and technology happens so rapidly, that we are constantly faced with the choice of making changes to up grade. The worlds' economy is relentless in pushing its programs of abuse and false promises. For us to break this cycle of abuse and false promises, we must involve God in our lives.

In the lives of those in the stories told, we can see just how involving God made a real difference in their lives in changing how they handled the resources He entrusted to them. However, for many of us, making that change is very difficult. We live in a society that teaches us to worship people, things, places, and circumstances and for many, especially African-Americans this worshipping hinders all efforts in making a real change. We have been taught to live a life of debt and feel good about it. But really, does it really feel good—does money really love you? I love money, but does money love me? This is another question we should all ask ourselves!

Now this brings me to our next step, getting wisdom! This step is very critical and I can't say enough about it, except that you will not have any success in moving towards financial freedom without it. Look around you, there are hundreds of families who have stopped living in debt from paycheck to paycheck–they all realized it was just plain stupid living. These people can tell you how their lives were changed through using the wisdom of others–they read books by *Lee Jenkins, Dave Ramsey, Howard Dayton, Suzy Orman* and other well known financial counselors. What these individuals have to say can really change ones way of thinking. They all give good sound practical steps to follow–steps to help you move from being in debt to being financially free. They talk about earnings, spending, saving, investing, and giving.

King Solomon, one of the greatest kings in the bible went to Gibeon to offer a sacrifice. He went there because it was the most important place of worship. While he was at Gibeon, the Lord came to him in a dream during the night. God said, "Ask for anything you want. I will give it to you. Solomon answered, "Lord my God, you have allowed me to be king in my father's place. But I am like a little child. I do not have the wisdom I need to do what I must do. I, your servant am here among your chosen people. There are too many of them to count. So I ask that you give me wisdom. Then I can rule the people in the right way. Then I will know the difference between right and wrong. Without wisdom, it is impossible to rule this great people of yours." The Lord was pleased that Solomon asked him for this. So God said to him, since you asked for wisdom to make the right decisions, I will give you what you asked. I will give you wisdom and understanding. The rest of the story is known to many of us; Solomon became the wisest and richest man to walk the face of the earth. Would God not do it for you, if only you asked? [7]

Only the Lord gives wisdom.
Knowledge and understanding come from Him.
Proverbs 2:6

Our new president, Barack Obama is still a stranger to most of us. He is seeking wisdom to turn a very bad economy around. In getting real transparency as he so desire, he could come before the public and say;

> *"Friends, this thing is a lot worse then I thought. Just like many of you, we are way over our budget. Some of you brought houses you couldn't afford. Many of you spent more money than you made and put the stuff you couldn't afford on your credit cards. The banks were irresponsible, and Wall Street was greedy, but I have to admit to you, the guys and gals over in the Congress have been spending at record rates, too. So, what are we to do?" This is a question that should be asked and pondered by all.*

You see, putting honesty in ones thoughts and character is a virtue. Wisdom too is also a virtue that one should seek and possess to effectively solve problems and challenges as they present themselves. Wisdom is like a person calling out to you. It says:

> *"Listen! I have important things to say, what I tell you are right, what I say is true! People with good sense know what I say is true! People with knowledge know that my words are right."*
> Proverbs 8:6-9

I believe most of us are in a financial mess simply because we never sought wisdom. However, there are some who did seek wisdom and as a result was greatly rewarded. Let's take a look at a couple of these success stories.

Nichole J's story:

> *"As of a week ago, our family has joined the ranks of the unemployed and thus uninsured. We have two children, a 6 year old and a 10 month old. With my part-time job and unemployment, we should be able to keep the roof over our heads, at least one car in the driveway, and food in our stomachs for a few months, or until we are fully employed again. To say we have no concerns would be untrue;*

however, we trust the Lord to do His part. We are doing our part in planning and budgeting. No one plans on being unemployed, but living God's plan does make for a lot easier time."

Milton and Kimberly N's story:

Milton was laid off a very high paying position as a law partner in one of the top law firms in the city of Atlanta, but because of using good wisdom, living on less than he made, saving, budgeting, and staying out of debt (owing only on their home)—living God's plan, they have no fears of surviving until he is once again employed full-time. He and his family did cut back on some of their spending, but they are contented.

These are just two examples of families taking advantage of wisdom in handling their finances. There are many more and I'm sure you too also know of families and individuals who have taken advantage of God's wisdom. Prayerfully you are or soon will be one of them.

OK! You ask where I get this wisdom you are talking about. Well first you know I'm going to direct you to the wisdom of God, because he's the architect and author of it all, He's the creator and who better knows how it works and how to handle the resources. He encourages us through his word to seek his counsel. His word says:

"A man without wisdom enjoys being foolish.
But a man with understanding does what is right."
Proverbs 15:21

Now it seems to me that we all have a choice when it comes to handling our resources, we can be foolish or wise. Although God has a bunch to say about handling his resources given to us, He will not force us to listen, what will force us, in most cases, is our circumstances. But, I'll get right to the point, seek God's wisdom, read His word, and commit to doing what He says to do with the resources (money) He gives to you.

Another source of wisdom is that of Godly people who are living according to God's commands when it comes to handling money. These are people who live by God's principles, who live on less than they make, people who are generous givers, people who live in God's kingdom and not the world's kingdom. And, really, they do have fun and enjoy life! Many started out in financial bondage, but took the steps to change. They realized God had good news for them in His word as to ways in handling and managing His money. They took the steps to learn through study in Crown Ministries and Total Money Makeover. They sought Godly counsel, set goals, made plans, and lived simple, sacrificially, and sincerely. God prospered them and made them successful so that they are now in the position to help other. There are a growing number of people, African-Americans included, that have a story to tell and to share. Chad and Pam are just one of many. Here's their story:

Chad and Pam's story:

> *Chad and Pam have a total annual income of just over $100,000, live on a monthly spending plan (not without some challenges), have an emergency fund established, owe only on their home, have no other debts (when a credit card is used, it is paid in full each billing), have money saved, and are very generous with their giving. Guess what, they travel and do the things in life that bring meaning and joy to them like short-term mission trips (vacations with a purpose)—they don't buy a whole lot of stuff.*

Not only do Chad and Pam adhere to God's word, they also seek Godly counsel in form of classes and discussions with others who have the same desires as they do.

> *Those who always respect the Lord will be happy.*
> *But those who are stubborn will get into trouble.*
> Proverbs 28:14

Smart people want more knowledge.
But a foolish person just wants more foolishness.
Proverbs 15:14

Chad and Pam are a growing number of African-Americans who are changing their ways and thoughts when it comes to handling their money and resources. However, there are far too many who have not made the change and continue to live a mundane, frustrating day to day same old depressing lifestyle in making a living for themselves and their families. Sad to say, we all probably know of many more in this condition–maybe even including ourselves, than those of the Chad and Pam category. Let's just take one area to discuss. Chad and Pam do not drive brand new cars, their cars are three to four years old and paid in full and yet they travel from point A to point B stress free and in comfort. But, because so many African-Americans are caught up or captured by the theory of "planned obsolescence" and "technological advancement", they must have brand new cars with high monthly payments. Yes, they do ride in comfort and style and get from point A to point B stress free (except for maybe the stress of making car payments). But then, are not a growing number of individuals doing the same with slightly older cars and NO monthly car notes?

The rich rule over the poor.
And borrowers become servants to those who lend.
Proverbs 22:7

We covet things and push to get ahead simply because we are never satisfied with what we have and have not learned to let loose the world and everything in it. You know it is not that you shouldn't have a new car, or that it is wrong to have one, but the problem is that we for the most part cannot be contented with what we have until such time as we can afford the new one. *Matthew Henry* says. *"Whatever you have of the world in your hands, keep it out of your heart."* Now I think this is a great statement and should be internalized by all.

A greedy person brings trouble to his family.
But the person who can't be paid to do wrong will live.
Proverbs 15:27

The last point I want to talk about is "getting real with ones situation."

Then Jesus said to the people, *"When you see clouds coming up in the west, you say, it's going to rain." And soon it begins to rain. When you feel the wind begin to blow from the south, you say, "It will be a hot day." And you are right. Hypocrites! You can understand the weather. Why don't you understand what is happening now!"*[8]

Kyle had spent long hours encouraging and discussing with his younger brother Bobby to change his habits on how he handle his resources and money, but to no avail, Bobby always rebuffed him with the statement that all was find—"just have to pay off this last bill and I'll be in good shape to start saving and living a better life." But, it never happens and out of their last conversation, Bobby asked Kyle to loan him money to keep the lights on in his apartment. Now I ask you, "does it seem as if things will get better anytime soon with Bobby?" With his present way of thinking, I don't think so!

This is a classic example of how so many African-Americans hide from the reality of their true state of financial being. Here was an example of what NOT being real looks like. My friend, you are NOT in good financial shape if you are living from paycheck to paycheck, head over heels in debt, and have no savings! Wake up to the fact that living in financial bondage is not contentment, but extremely stressful.

On the other hand, because of the financial situation in today's United States, (job losses, foreclosures, lack of credit, rising gas prices) more and more African-Americans are turning to experts to help them get out of the financial mess they find themselves in. Most of the experts have great knowledge and facts to share in helping them. They can help focus individuals in acknowledging that they do have a financial problem, and should do something about it. I believe this is the start of getting real—acknowledging the problem!

Foolish people hate wisdom and self-control.
Proverbs 1:7b

Let's say you do recognize a problem and decide to do something about it. Most African-Americans start out to do something about their problem, but I must say this, they quickly fall into one or several roadblocks. If you are not prepared for them, they can easily defeat you and shut down whatever plans you may have had. Some of these roadblocks are auto repairs, medical bills, unexpected expenses, and so on. There are many roadblocks, and you can now understand why so many give up on changing their financial situation. It took time for you to get into your mess–probably months or even years, so please don't expect to get out of it with ease or quickness. It could take some real trying times and maybe months to do so! The enemy love to see you in financial bondage, and so will do all he can to hinder you from following through with your plans. You need to have a really solid plan–a plan birth out of good counsel and much prayer. You need a strong track to run on and a team of encouragers and accountability partners. Even with a good plan developed, you need to be able to make adjustments–rarely will a plan move to completion without some adjustments being made. However, taking all of this into account you do recognize the problem, you seek wise counsel, decide on a plan, and act on it swiftly and firmly. Most importantly, you have the Lord as your chief counselor. Once you arrive at this point, you are now ready to implement the steps needed in formulating you plan.

Remember, God has designated the most difficult first step, transfer of ownership to Him. Once this has been accomplished, all other steps will fall into place. Accept God's counsel and recognize that His counsel is what He gives to provide direction in our lives. Remember, His counsel is also given through Godly men and women. Their counsel is invaluable. There are many programs, classes, and resources available to all who desire help, but I won't go into any of them here, because my purpose for writing this book is to get you to the point of knowing **why** you should make a change in your thinking.

Your commands make me wiser than my enemies (world's economy)
because they are mine forever.
I am wiser than all my teachers because I think about your rules
(God's economy).
I have more understanding than the older leaders because
I follow your orders.
I have avoided every evil way so I could obey your word.
I haven't stopped obeying your laws because
you yourself are my teacher.
Your promises are so sweet to me. They are like honey to my mouth!
Psalm 119:98-103

Those who struggle with their financial well-being will really benefit from meditating on these verses. God is telling us that His commands and ways are true and lead to prosperity and success. The ways of the world, can not say the same!

Who has measured the oceans in the palm of his hand?
Who has used his hand to measure the sky?
Who has used a bowl to measure all the dust of the earth?
Who has used scales to weight the mountains and hills?
Who has known the mind of the Lord?
Who has been able to give the Lord advice?
Whom did the Lord ask for help?
Who taught him the right way?
Who taught the Lord knowledge?
Who showed him the way to understanding?
Isaiah 40:12-14

Good sense will protect you.
Understanding will guard you.
Proverb 2:11

CONCLUSION

THESE ARE TOUGH economic times, especially for African-Americans with higher rates of unemployment (currently over 17%), income disparity, and credit discrimination. These are just a few financial impediments to the economic vitality of African-Americans, but so are their consumer habits and tastes. Alarmingly, rather than cutting back on spending, the response has been to spend more. Many find themselves in deep trouble, because they live above their heads. Once they get into that way of living, it's hard to stop, even it they are living paycheck to paycheck. Don't get me wrong, I don't say this about everyone, but for a lot of people, this shortsighted behavior, motivated by a desire for instant gratification and social acceptance, comes at a great expense–our future! I pray that your mind is made up and you will seek Godly wisdom and counsel to help you track your income and spending. I pray that you set up a spending plan (budget), start a saving and start paying off all of your debts. Become the giver that God wants you to be. You may love money, but does money really love you?

God's wisdom is so much more powerful than the world's wisdom! He understands the way to wisdom. And He is the only one who knows where it lives. However, taking these steps is meaningless if your attitude and relationship with your resources have not changed—you may go through the motions but you will do so without any lasting changes.

In the book of Job, despite his confusion and pain, Job makes it clear that he looks to God alone for wisdom. He understands that he cannot lead himself, much less his family, without God as his never-ending source of perspective and understanding. His friends and his wife tried their best to get him to change his mind, but Job was not satisfied until he had the wisdom of God.[9]

I want to tell you about an African folk tale. It's about the Mushroom and goes like this:

> *"Once there was a Mushroom in the middle of the world, and all the animals were on one side and all the good food of the world on the other side. The Mushroom said to the animals, "If all of you will break me down, you may go by and get all the food." And so the animals came to try. Elephant was the first to try. The Mushroom killed him and threw him into the sea. Reindeer and Hippopotamus came, but couldn't throw it down. So Turtle came to try. He went one day and ate half the stalk of it. Another day, he ate the other half. Then the top of the Mushroom fell. Then all the animals crossed to the other side, and lived there forever afterward."[10]*

The moral of the story is: Always tackle the stalk of difficulty. Then, the top topples. Put another way; tough decisions are made by attacking the root of the problem.

It is important for us to realize that God controls and uses even difficult circumstances for good in the life of those who love him and are yielded to him as Lord.

God is waiting for you to make that decision, to seek His wisdom. The fear of the Lord is wisdom, and to stay away from evil is understanding.

A wise person is known for his understanding.
Proverbs 16:21a

Depend on the Lord in whatever you do.
Then your plans will succeed.
Proverbs 16:3

I pray this small book have stirred in you a desire to really make a radical change in your attitude and relationship with the resources entrusted to you–to seek God first in your life, to seek his wisdom, to get real with your circumstances and start living a joyful debt free and more abundant life. I've been told by some that I don't go into the "how" to turn things around, again my focus here is to get you to change your thinking, to understand the "why." However, I realize the "perfect financial storm" is approaching quickly. We, as Christians, need to be prepared to ride it out. So to weather the approaching storm, here are a few steps we should take:

- Be prepared–know and understand the current economic times.
- Get out of debt–Eliminate all debts.
- Tithe–Trust in God.
- Gain knowledge–Know your circumstances, strengthen yourself in the Lord, focus on what you have and can do, and always inquire of the Lord.

I firmly believe no real action happens until a person firmly knows why and believes in the change he or she is about to make. It is really God's desire that we live a life of contentment, a life of joyful giving. Sometimes we are so absorbed with "getting what's ours" that we miss out on what brings the real blessing and joy–giving to God. Giving is what we were made for. It is an act that leads to a joyful life. Become the generous giver God wants you to be, have the faith and trust God wants you to have to believe that he will take care of ALL your needs and MOST of your wants and desires.

. . . It is more blessed to give than to receive.
Acts 20:35

ENDNOTES

1. Consumer Federation of America; survey report of August 29, 2002 showing the economic position of African-Americans.
2. Black americaweb.com; the color of money column. Vehicle Loans–the lowdown. April 27, 2007
3. Consumer Federation of America; survey report of October 29, 2003 showing the economic position of African-Americans.
4. Summary of selected scriptures from 1Samuel 3:1-19, The Everyday Bible.
5. Consumer Federation of America; survey report of October 29, 2003 showing spending habits of African-Americans.
6. Summary of Ezra working hard and obeying God from Ezra 7:10, The Everyday Bible.
7. Summary of King Solomon's request of God from 1Kings 3:4-14, The Everyday Bible.
8. Summary of the Lord's challenge to the people in Luke 12:54-56, The Everyday Bible.
9. Summary of Job's dialog with God from Job 42:1-6, The Everyday Bible.
10. African Folk Tales as told to Dr Pauline E Jenkins